50 Bangladesh Recipes for Home

By: Kelly Johnson

Table of Contents

- Biryani
- Fish curry
- Panta bhat
- Chingri malai curry
- Dal
- Shorshe ilish
- Pitha
- Bhuna khichuri
- Fuchka
- Bhapa pitha
- Beef bhuna
- Chomchom
- Pati shapta
- Mishti doi
- Morog polao
- Bhapa doi
- Sandesh
- Shutki
- Jhal muri
- Roshogolla
- Luchi
- Bhaji
- Chotpoti
- Korma
- Piyaju
- Bhapa chingri
- Shobji bhorta
- Prawn curry
- Doi maach
- Shingara
- Borhani
- Khichuri
- Beef rezala
- Piyajoo pitha
- Malai curry

- Pati shapta
- Chanar payesh
- Chicken rezala
- Dhokar dalna
- Jorda pulao
- Kathal curry
- Kochu shak
- Lalmohon
- Matha
- Murighonto
- Narkel narus
- Patisapta
- Sarson shorshe ilish
- Shahi tukda
- Sukto

Biryani

Ingredients:

- 2 cups basmati rice, rinsed and soaked for 30 minutes
- 500g chicken, cut into pieces
- 1 large onion, thinly sliced
- 1/2 cup plain yogurt
- 2 tomatoes, chopped
- 2 tablespoons ginger-garlic paste
- 2 green chilies, slit lengthwise
- 1/4 cup chopped mint leaves
- 1/4 cup chopped coriander leaves
- 1 teaspoon cumin seeds
- 4-5 whole cloves
- 4-5 whole green cardamom pods
- 1-inch cinnamon stick
- 1 bay leaf
- 1/4 teaspoon saffron threads, soaked in 2 tablespoons warm milk
- 3 tablespoons ghee or vegetable oil
- Salt to taste

Instructions:

1. Heat ghee or oil in a large pot over medium heat. Add the sliced onions and fry until golden brown. Remove half of the fried onions and set aside for garnishing.
2. To the remaining onions in the pot, add the cumin seeds, cloves, cardamom pods, cinnamon stick, and bay leaf. Sauté for a minute until fragrant.
3. Add the ginger-garlic paste and green chilies. Cook for 2-3 minutes until the raw smell disappears.
4. Add the chopped tomatoes and cook until they turn mushy.
5. Add the chicken pieces and cook until they are no longer pink on the outside.
6. Stir in the yogurt, mint leaves, coriander leaves, and salt. Mix well to combine.
7. Drain the soaked rice and add it to the pot. Mix gently to combine with the chicken and spices.
8. Pour enough water into the pot to just cover the rice. Bring to a boil, then reduce the heat to low. Cover the pot with a tight-fitting lid and let the biryani simmer for 15-20 minutes, or until the rice is cooked and the chicken is tender.

9. Once the biryani is cooked, drizzle the saffron milk over the top and garnish with the reserved fried onions.
10. Serve hot with raita (yogurt sauce) and your favorite pickles.

Enjoy your delicious homemade Chicken Biryani!

Fish curry

Ingredients:

- 500g fish fillets (such as rohu, hilsa, or tilapia)
- 2 onions, finely chopped
- 2 tomatoes, finely chopped
- 2 green chilies, slit lengthwise
- 3 cloves garlic, minced
- 1-inch ginger, grated
- 1 teaspoon turmeric powder
- 1 teaspoon red chili powder
- 1 teaspoon coriander powder
- 1/2 teaspoon cumin powder
- 1/2 teaspoon mustard seeds
- 1/2 teaspoon fenugreek seeds
- 2-3 dry red chilies
- 1 bay leaf
- 1 cinnamon stick
- 2-3 cloves
- 2-3 cardamom pods
- 1 cup coconut milk
- 2 tablespoons mustard oil or vegetable oil
- Salt to taste
- Fresh coriander leaves for garnish

Instructions:

1. Clean and wash the fish fillets. Pat them dry with paper towels and sprinkle with a pinch of turmeric and salt. Set aside.
2. Heat mustard oil or vegetable oil in a large pan or kadhai over medium heat.
3. Add mustard seeds, fenugreek seeds, dry red chilies, bay leaf, cinnamon stick, cloves, and cardamom pods. Sauté for a minute until the spices release their aroma.
4. Add the chopped onions and sauté until they turn golden brown.
5. Add the minced garlic and grated ginger. Sauté for another couple of minutes until the raw smell disappears.

6. Stir in the turmeric powder, red chili powder, coriander powder, and cumin powder. Cook for a minute until the spices are fragrant.
7. Add the chopped tomatoes and green chilies. Cook until the tomatoes are soft and mashed.
8. Pour in the coconut milk and bring the mixture to a simmer.
9. Gently slide in the fish fillets into the simmering curry. Spoon some of the curry sauce over the fish to coat.
10. Cover the pan and let the fish cook in the curry for about 10-15 minutes, or until the fish is cooked through and flakes easily with a fork.
11. Once the fish is cooked, check the seasoning and adjust salt if needed.
12. Garnish with fresh coriander leaves and serve hot with steamed rice.

Enjoy your flavorful Bengali-style Fish Curry!

Panta bhat

Ingredients:

- 1 cup parboiled rice (preferably short-grain)
- 2-3 cups water
- Salt to taste
- Optional: sliced onions, green chilies, fried fish, pickles, or yogurt for serving

Instructions:

1. Rinse the rice thoroughly under cold water until the water runs clear. Drain the rice and transfer it to a bowl.
2. Add enough water to fully submerge the rice, about 2-3 cups. Allow the rice to soak in the water for at least 8-10 hours or overnight.
3. After soaking, the rice will have absorbed most of the water and become swollen.
4. In a separate pot, bring water to a boil. Add a pinch of salt to the boiling water.
5. Once the water is boiling, add the soaked rice to the pot. Cook the rice over medium heat, stirring occasionally, until it becomes soft and mushy. This usually takes about 20-30 minutes.
6. Once the rice is cooked, remove it from the heat and allow it to cool to room temperature.
7. Once cooled, mash the rice gently with the back of a spoon to achieve a slightly coarse texture. The consistency should be similar to porridge.
8. Transfer the mashed rice to a clean bowl and cover it with a lid or plastic wrap. Allow the rice to ferment at room temperature for at least 6-8 hours or overnight. During fermentation, the rice will develop a slightly sour flavor.
9. After fermentation, serve the Panta Bhat chilled or at room temperature, accompanied by sliced onions, green chilies, fried fish, pickles, or yogurt according to your preference.

Enjoy the refreshing and nutritious taste of Panta Bhat, a beloved dish in Bengali cuisine!

Chingri malai curry

Ingredients:

- 500g large prawns, cleaned and deveined
- 1 cup coconut milk
- 1 large onion, finely chopped
- 2 tomatoes, finely chopped
- 2 green chilies, slit lengthwise
- 3 cloves garlic, minced
- 1-inch ginger, grated
- 1 teaspoon turmeric powder
- 1 teaspoon red chili powder
- 1 teaspoon cumin powder
- 1/2 teaspoon sugar
- 2-3 tablespoons mustard oil or vegetable oil
- Salt to taste
- Fresh coriander leaves for garnish

Instructions:

1. Heat mustard oil or vegetable oil in a large pan or kadhai over medium heat.
2. Add the chopped onions and sauté until they turn golden brown.
3. Add the minced garlic and grated ginger. Sauté for another couple of minutes until the raw smell disappears.
4. Stir in the turmeric powder, red chili powder, and cumin powder. Cook for a minute until the spices are fragrant.
5. Add the chopped tomatoes and green chilies. Cook until the tomatoes are soft and mashed.
6. Add the cleaned prawns to the pan and stir well to coat them with the spice mixture.
7. Cook the prawns for 2-3 minutes until they turn pink and opaque.
8. Pour in the coconut milk and stir to combine. Add salt to taste and a pinch of sugar to balance the flavors.
9. Let the curry simmer for 5-7 minutes until the prawns are fully cooked and the gravy thickens slightly.
10. Once the prawns are cooked through, remove the pan from heat.
11. Garnish the Chingri Malai Curry with fresh coriander leaves.

12. Serve hot with steamed rice or your favorite bread.

Enjoy the rich and creamy goodness of Chingri Malai Curry, a delightful delicacy from Bengali cuisine!

Dal

Ingredients:

- 1 cup red lentils (masoor dal), washed and drained
- 3 cups water
- 1 onion, finely chopped
- 2 tomatoes, finely chopped
- 3 cloves garlic, minced
- 1-inch ginger, grated
- 2 green chilies, slit lengthwise
- 1 teaspoon turmeric powder
- 1 teaspoon cumin seeds
- 1 teaspoon mustard seeds
- 1 dried red chili
- 2-3 tablespoons mustard oil or vegetable oil
- Salt to taste
- Fresh coriander leaves for garnish

Instructions:

1. In a large pot or pressure cooker, combine the washed lentils and water. Bring to a boil over medium-high heat.
2. Once boiling, reduce the heat to low and simmer the lentils, partially covered, for about 20-25 minutes or until they are soft and mushy. Stir occasionally to prevent sticking.
3. While the lentils are cooking, heat mustard oil or vegetable oil in a separate pan over medium heat.
4. Add the cumin seeds, mustard seeds, and dried red chili to the hot oil. Sauté for a minute until the seeds start to crackle.
5. Add the chopped onions to the pan and sauté until they turn golden brown.
6. Stir in the minced garlic, grated ginger, and green chilies. Sauté for another couple of minutes until the raw smell disappears.
7. Add the turmeric powder to the pan and cook for a minute until fragrant.
8. Add the chopped tomatoes to the pan and cook until they are soft and mashed.
9. Once the lentils are cooked, add the cooked onion-tomato mixture to the pot of lentils. Mix well to combine.

10. Season the dal with salt to taste and let it simmer for another 5-10 minutes to allow the flavors to meld together.
11. Garnish the Dal with fresh coriander leaves before serving.
12. Serve hot with steamed rice or your favorite bread.

Enjoy the comforting and nutritious goodness of Bangladeshi-style Dal!

Shorshe ilish

Ingredients:

- 4 pieces of hilsa fish (ilish)
- 4 tablespoons mustard paste (made by grinding yellow mustard seeds with water)
- 2 green chilies, slit lengthwise
- 1 teaspoon turmeric powder
- 1 tablespoon mustard oil
- Salt to taste
- Fresh coriander leaves for garnish

Instructions:

1. Clean the hilsa fish pieces thoroughly and pat them dry with paper towels.
2. Rub the fish pieces with turmeric powder and a little salt. Let them marinate for about 15-20 minutes.
3. Heat mustard oil in a pan over medium heat.
4. Once the oil is hot, carefully place the marinated fish pieces in the pan. Fry them on both sides until they turn golden brown. Remove the fish pieces from the pan and set them aside.
5. In the same pan, add the green chilies and sauté for a minute.
6. Add the mustard paste to the pan and cook for 2-3 minutes, stirring constantly.
7. Gradually add water to the mustard paste while stirring continuously to prevent lumps from forming. Adjust the consistency of the gravy according to your preference.
8. Add salt to taste and stir well to combine.
9. Gently slide the fried fish pieces into the mustard gravy, making sure they are fully submerged.
10. Cover the pan and let the fish simmer in the gravy for about 5-7 minutes, allowing the flavors to meld together.
11. Once the fish is cooked through and the gravy reaches your desired consistency, remove the pan from heat.
12. Garnish the Shorshe Ilish with fresh coriander leaves before serving.
13. Serve hot with steamed rice.

Enjoy the delightful flavors of Shorshe Ilish, a quintessential Bengali delicacy!

Pitha

Ingredients:

- 1 cup rice flour
- 1/2 cup water
- 1/4 teaspoon salt
- 1 tablespoon sugar
- Vegetable oil for frying

Instructions:

1. In a mixing bowl, combine the rice flour, salt, and sugar. Gradually add water while stirring continuously to form a smooth batter. The consistency should be thick but pourable.
2. Heat a non-stick frying pan or tawa over medium heat. Lightly grease the surface with oil.
3. Pour a ladleful of the batter onto the hot pan and spread it thinly into a round shape using the back of the ladle. The pitha should be about 6-7 inches in diameter.
4. Cook the pitha for 2-3 minutes on one side until it starts to bubble and the edges turn golden brown.
5. Flip the pitha and cook for another 1-2 minutes on the other side until cooked through and lightly browned.
6. Remove the cooked pitha from the pan and place it on a plate. Repeat the process with the remaining batter.
7. Once all the pithas are cooked, allow them to cool slightly before serving.
8. Serve the Chitoi Pitha warm with your favorite accompaniments such as grated coconut, jaggery syrup, or sweetened condensed milk.

Enjoy the delicious and comforting taste of Chitoi Pitha, a delightful treat from Bengali cuisine!

Bhuna khichuri

Ingredients:

- 1 cup basmati rice
- 1/2 cup yellow moong dal (split mung beans)
- 1 onion, finely chopped
- 2 tomatoes, finely chopped
- 2-3 green chilies, slit lengthwise
- 2 cloves garlic, minced
- 1-inch ginger, grated
- 1 teaspoon turmeric powder
- 1 teaspoon cumin seeds
- 1 teaspoon coriander powder
- 1/2 teaspoon red chili powder (adjust to taste)
- 1/2 teaspoon garam masala powder
- 2 tablespoons ghee or vegetable oil
- Salt to taste
- Fresh coriander leaves for garnish
- Optional: fried onions for garnish

Instructions:

1. Rinse the basmati rice and yellow moong dal under cold water until the water runs clear. Drain well and set aside.
2. Heat ghee or vegetable oil in a pressure cooker or deep pot over medium heat.
3. Add the cumin seeds and allow them to splutter.
4. Add the chopped onions and sauté until they turn golden brown.
5. Stir in the minced garlic and grated ginger. Sauté for another couple of minutes until fragrant.
6. Add the chopped tomatoes and green chilies. Cook until the tomatoes are soft and mashed.
7. Add the turmeric powder, coriander powder, red chili powder, and salt. Mix well to combine.
8. Add the rinsed rice and dal to the pot. Stir to coat them with the spice mixture.
9. Pour in about 3 cups of water and mix well.

10. Close the pressure cooker lid and cook the khichuri over medium heat for about 3-4 whistles, or if using a pot, cook covered until the rice and dal are cooked through and soft. Stir occasionally to prevent sticking.
11. Once the khichuri is cooked, sprinkle garam masala powder over it and mix gently.
12. Garnish with fresh coriander leaves and fried onions (if using).
13. Serve hot Bhuna Khichuri with your favorite accompaniments such as fried eggplant slices, papad, or a dollop of yogurt.

Enjoy the comforting and flavorful Bhuna Khichuri, perfect for a cozy meal!

Fuchka

Ingredients:

For the puris:

- 1 cup semolina (sooji)
- 1/4 cup all-purpose flour (maida)
- Water, as needed
- Vegetable oil for frying

For the filling:

- 2 medium potatoes, boiled and mashed
- 1 cup boiled chickpeas
- 1 onion, finely chopped
- 2 green chilies, finely chopped
- 1/4 cup chopped coriander leaves
- 1 teaspoon chaat masala
- 1/2 teaspoon roasted cumin powder
- Salt to taste

For the tamarind water:

- 1/4 cup tamarind pulp
- 2 cups water
- 1 teaspoon chaat masala
- 1/2 teaspoon black salt
- 1/2 teaspoon roasted cumin powder
- 1/4 teaspoon red chili powder (optional)
- Salt to taste

Instructions:

1. To make the puris, mix together semolina and all-purpose flour in a bowl. Gradually add water and knead into a stiff dough. Cover with a damp cloth and let it rest for 15-20 minutes.

2. Divide the dough into small portions and roll each portion into a small ball. Roll out each ball into a thin circle, about 2-3 inches in diameter.
3. Heat vegetable oil in a deep frying pan over medium heat. Fry the puris in batches until they puff up and turn golden brown. Remove from oil and drain on paper towels.
4. To prepare the filling, mix together mashed potatoes, boiled chickpeas, chopped onion, green chilies, coriander leaves, chaat masala, roasted cumin powder, and salt in a bowl. Adjust seasoning to taste.
5. To make the tamarind water, mix tamarind pulp with water in a bowl. Add chaat masala, black salt, roasted cumin powder, red chili powder (if using), and salt. Stir well to combine.
6. To assemble the Fuchka, gently make a hole in the center of each puri using your thumb. Fill each puri with the potato-chickpea mixture.
7. Dip the filled puris in the tamarind water and place them on a serving plate.
8. Serve immediately and enjoy the burst of flavors in each bite!

Fuchka is best enjoyed fresh and can be customized with additional toppings such as sweet chutney, spicy chutney, or sev according to personal preference.

Bhapa pitha

Ingredients:

- 1 cup rice flour
- 1/2 cup grated coconut
- 1/2 cup jaggery (or sugar)
- 1/2 cup water
- 1/4 teaspoon cardamom powder
- 1/4 teaspoon salt
- Banana leaves or parchment paper for steaming

Instructions:

1. In a mixing bowl, combine rice flour, grated coconut, jaggery (or sugar), cardamom powder, and salt. Mix well.
2. Gradually add water while stirring continuously to form a smooth batter. The consistency should be thick but pourable.
3. Cut the banana leaves into small squares and lightly grease them with oil. If using parchment paper, cut it into squares and set aside.
4. Pour the batter into the greased banana leaves or parchment paper, filling each about halfway.
5. Fold the banana leaves or parchment paper to enclose the batter, forming small parcels or packets.
6. Prepare a steamer by bringing water to a boil in a large pot or steamer.
7. Once the water is boiling, place the Bhapa Pitha packets in the steamer basket, ensuring they are not overcrowded.
8. Cover the steamer with a lid and steam the Bhapa Pitha for about 15-20 minutes, or until they are cooked through and firm to the touch.
9. Remove the Bhapa Pitha from the steamer and let them cool slightly before serving.
10. Unwrap the Bhapa Pitha from the banana leaves or parchment paper and serve warm or at room temperature.

Enjoy the delicious and aromatic Bhapa Pitha as a delightful treat during festivities or as a sweet snack!

Beef bhuna

Ingredients:

- 500g beef, cut into cubes
- 2 onions, finely chopped
- 2 tomatoes, finely chopped
- 3 cloves garlic, minced
- 1-inch ginger, grated
- 2 green chilies, slit lengthwise
- 2 tablespoons plain yogurt
- 1 tablespoon tomato paste
- 1 teaspoon turmeric powder
- 2 teaspoons cumin powder
- 2 teaspoons coriander powder
- 1 teaspoon red chili powder (adjust to taste)
- 1/2 teaspoon garam masala powder
- 1/2 teaspoon black pepper powder
- 1/4 cup vegetable oil
- Salt to taste
- Fresh coriander leaves for garnish

Instructions:

1. Heat vegetable oil in a deep pan or kadhai over medium heat.
2. Add the chopped onions and sauté until they turn golden brown.
3. Add the minced garlic and grated ginger. Sauté for another couple of minutes until fragrant.
4. Stir in the chopped tomatoes and green chilies. Cook until the tomatoes are soft and mashed.
5. Add the turmeric powder, cumin powder, coriander powder, red chili powder, black pepper powder, and salt. Mix well to combine.
6. Add the beef cubes to the pan and stir to coat them with the spice mixture.
7. Cook the beef over medium heat, stirring occasionally, until it is browned on all sides.
8. Once the beef is browned, reduce the heat to low and cover the pan. Let the beef cook slowly for about 1 to 1.5 hours, or until it is tender and cooked through. Stir occasionally and add a little water if needed to prevent sticking.

9. Once the beef is cooked and the oil starts to separate from the masala, add the plain yogurt and tomato paste. Mix well to combine.
10. Cook the beef for another 10-15 minutes, stirring occasionally, until the masala thickens and coats the beef.
11. Sprinkle garam masala powder over the beef bhuna and mix well.
12. Garnish with fresh coriander leaves before serving.
13. Serve hot with steamed rice or your favorite bread.

Enjoy the rich and aromatic flavors of Beef Bhuna, a classic Bangladeshi delicacy!

Chomchom

Ingredients:

For the Chomchom:

- 1 liter full-fat milk
- 2 tablespoons lemon juice or vinegar
- 1 cup sugar
- A pinch of saffron strands
- 4-5 green cardamom pods, crushed
- 2 cups water
- Silver leaf (optional, for garnish)
- Chopped nuts (such as pistachios or almonds) for garnish

For the sugar syrup:

- 2 cups water
- 2 cups sugar
- 2-3 drops rose water or kewra water (optional)

Instructions:

1. Start by making the paneer (Indian cottage cheese). In a large pot, bring the milk to a gentle boil over medium heat.
2. Once the milk starts boiling, reduce the heat to low and add lemon juice or vinegar gradually, stirring continuously, until the milk curdles and separates into curds (paneer) and whey.
3. Line a colander with cheesecloth and pour the curdled milk into it. Rinse the paneer under cold water to remove the lemony taste.
4. Gather the corners of the cheesecloth and squeeze out any excess water from the paneer. Hang the cheesecloth for about 30 minutes to drain any remaining liquid.
5. Transfer the drained paneer to a large plate or bowl. Knead the paneer with the heel of your hand until it becomes smooth and soft. This will take about 7-10 minutes.
6. Divide the paneer dough into equal-sized portions and shape each portion into cylindrical or oval-shaped dumplings (Chomchom).

7. In a wide pan, combine water, sugar, saffron strands, and crushed cardamom pods to make the sugar syrup. Bring it to a boil over medium heat.
8. Gently slide the paneer dumplings into the boiling sugar syrup. Cover the pan and cook the Chomchom for about 15-20 minutes, occasionally flipping them to ensure even cooking.
9. Once the Chomchom doubles in size and becomes spongy, turn off the heat and let them cool in the syrup for a while.
10. Once cooled, remove the Chomchom from the syrup and place them on a serving plate.
11. Garnish the Chomchom with chopped nuts and silver leaf (if using).
12. Serve Chomchom chilled or at room temperature, as a delightful dessert.

Enjoy the sweet and creamy indulgence of homemade Chomchom, a beloved treat in Bengali cuisine!

Pati shapta

Ingredients:

For the crepes:

- 1 cup all-purpose flour (maida)
- 1/2 cup semolina (sooji)
- 1 cup milk
- 1/2 cup water
- 2 tablespoons sugar
- A pinch of salt
- Ghee or vegetable oil for frying

For the filling:

- 1 cup grated coconut
- 1/2 cup khoya (reduced milk solids)
- 1/2 cup sugar
- 1/4 teaspoon cardamom powder
- 2 tablespoons chopped nuts (such as almonds or pistachios)
- 2 tablespoons raisins (optional)

For the thickened milk (optional):

- 2 cups milk
- 2 tablespoons sugar
- 1/4 teaspoon cardamom powder
- Chopped nuts for garnish

Instructions:

1. To make the crepes, combine all-purpose flour, semolina, milk, water, sugar, and a pinch of salt in a mixing bowl. Whisk until you get a smooth batter without any lumps. Let the batter rest for about 30 minutes.
2. In a separate bowl, prepare the filling by mixing together grated coconut, khoya, sugar, cardamom powder, chopped nuts, and raisins (if using). Set aside.

3. Heat a non-stick frying pan or tawa over medium heat. Lightly grease the surface with ghee or vegetable oil.
4. Pour a ladleful of the crepe batter onto the hot pan and spread it into a thin, round shape. Cook for about 1-2 minutes until the bottom side is golden brown and the top side is set.
5. Spoon a portion of the coconut-khoya filling along the center of the crepe. Fold the sides of the crepe over the filling to form a roll or fold it into a half-moon shape. Press gently to seal the edges.
6. Cook the filled crepe for another minute until it is lightly browned and crisp on both sides. Remove from the pan and set aside.
7. Repeat the process with the remaining batter and filling to make more Pati Shapta crepes.
8. If making thickened milk, pour milk into a saucepan and bring it to a simmer over medium-low heat. Add sugar and cardamom powder, and simmer until the milk reduces and thickens slightly.
9. To serve, drizzle the thickened milk over the Pati Shapta crepes and garnish with chopped nuts.
10. Serve Pati Shapta warm or chilled, as a delightful dessert.

Enjoy the sweet and indulgent flavors of homemade Pati Shapta, a beloved treat in Bengali cuisine!

Mishti doi

Ingredients:

- 1 liter full-fat milk
- 1/2 cup sugar
- 2 tablespoons yogurt (as a starter culture)

Instructions:

1. Pour the milk into a heavy-bottomed saucepan and bring it to a boil over medium heat. Stir occasionally to prevent the milk from sticking to the bottom of the pan.
2. Once the milk comes to a boil, reduce the heat to low and simmer it for about 30-40 minutes, stirring occasionally, until it reduces to about half its original volume. The milk should thicken slightly and develop a creamy consistency.
3. Add sugar to the thickened milk and stir until the sugar dissolves completely. Continue simmering the milk for another 10-15 minutes, stirring occasionally, until it thickens further and turns slightly golden in color.
4. Remove the saucepan from heat and let the milk cool to lukewarm temperature.
5. In a small bowl, mix 2 tablespoons of yogurt with a few tablespoons of the lukewarm milk to temper it. Stir well to combine.
6. Add the tempered yogurt mixture back into the saucepan with the remaining lukewarm milk. Mix well to combine.
7. Pour the milk-yogurt mixture into earthenware pots or any clean, heatproof containers.
8. Cover the containers with a lid or aluminum foil.
9. Place the containers in a warm place, such as inside an oven with the light on or in a warm corner of the kitchen, and let them ferment for about 6-8 hours, or until the yogurt sets and becomes firm.
10. Once the Mishti Doi is set, refrigerate it for a few hours to chill before serving.
11. Serve the chilled Mishti Doi as a refreshing dessert.

Enjoy the creamy and sweet goodness of homemade Mishti Doi, a quintessential Bengali delicacy!

Morog polao

Ingredients:

- 2 cups basmati rice, soaked for 30 minutes and drained
- 500g chicken, cut into pieces
- 2 onions, thinly sliced
- 1/2 cup plain yogurt
- 2 tomatoes, chopped
- 2 tablespoons ginger-garlic paste
- 2 green chilies, slit lengthwise
- 1/4 cup chopped mint leaves
- 1/4 cup chopped coriander leaves
- 1 teaspoon cumin seeds
- 4-5 whole cloves
- 4-5 whole green cardamom pods
- 1-inch cinnamon stick
- 1 bay leaf
- 1/4 teaspoon saffron threads, soaked in 2 tablespoons warm milk
- 3 tablespoons ghee or vegetable oil
- Salt to taste

Instructions:

1. Heat ghee or vegetable oil in a large pot over medium heat. Add the sliced onions and fry until golden brown. Remove half of the fried onions and set aside for garnishing.
2. To the remaining onions in the pot, add the cumin seeds, cloves, cardamom pods, cinnamon stick, and bay leaf. Sauté for a minute until the spices release their aroma.
3. Add the ginger-garlic paste and green chilies. Cook for 2-3 minutes until the raw smell disappears.
4. Add the chopped tomatoes and cook until they turn mushy.
5. Add the chicken pieces and cook until they are no longer pink on the outside.
6. Stir in the yogurt, mint leaves, coriander leaves, and salt. Mix well to combine.
7. Add the drained basmati rice to the pot. Mix gently to combine with the chicken and spices.

8. Pour enough water into the pot to just cover the rice. Bring to a boil, then reduce the heat to low. Cover the pot with a tight-fitting lid and let the polao simmer for 15-20 minutes, or until the rice is cooked and the chicken is tender.
9. Once the polao is cooked, drizzle the saffron milk over the top and garnish with the reserved fried onions.
10. Serve hot with raita (yogurt sauce) and your favorite pickles.

Enjoy the rich and aromatic Morog Polao, a delightful dish from Bengali cuisine!

Bhapi doi

Ingredients:

- 2 cups plain yogurt (strained to remove excess whey)
- 1 cup sweetened condensed milk
- 1/2 cup sugar (adjust to taste)
- 1/4 teaspoon cardamom powder
- A pinch of saffron strands (optional)
- Chopped nuts for garnish (such as pistachios or almonds)

Instructions:

1. Preheat your steamer or a large pot with a steaming rack over medium heat.
2. In a mixing bowl, combine the strained yogurt, sweetened condensed milk, sugar, cardamom powder, and saffron strands (if using). Mix well until smooth and creamy.
3. Pour the yogurt mixture into a heatproof dish or individual ramekins. Tap the dish gently to remove any air bubbles.
4. Cover the dish tightly with aluminum foil to prevent water from getting into the mixture during steaming.
5. Place the dish on the steaming rack inside the preheated steamer or pot. Steam for about 30-40 minutes, or until the Bhapa Doi is set and firm around the edges but still slightly jiggly in the center.
6. Once cooked, remove the dish from the steamer and let it cool to room temperature.
7. Refrigerate the Bhapa Doi for at least 4-6 hours, or overnight, to chill and set completely.
8. Before serving, garnish the Bhapa Doi with chopped nuts.
9. Serve chilled Bhapa Doi as a delightful dessert.

Enjoy the creamy and indulgent sweetness of homemade Bhapa Doi, a classic Bengali delicacy!

Sandesh

Ingredients:

- 2 cups fresh chhena (Indian cottage cheese)
- 1/2 cup powdered sugar (adjust to taste)
- 1/4 teaspoon cardamom powder (optional)
- A few saffron strands (optional)
- Chopped nuts for garnish (such as pistachios or almonds)
- Edible silver leaf (optional, for decoration)

Instructions:

1. In a mixing bowl, knead the fresh chhena until smooth and creamy. This may take about 5-7 minutes.
2. Add powdered sugar and cardamom powder to the chhena. Mix well until the sugar is fully incorporated and the mixture becomes smooth.
3. If using saffron, soak the saffron strands in a tablespoon of warm milk for a few minutes. Add the saffron-infused milk to the chhena mixture and mix well to distribute the color and flavor evenly.
4. Take a small portion of the chhena mixture and shape it into small round balls or flatten them slightly to form discs. You can also use molds to shape the Sandesh into various designs.
5. Garnish each Sandesh with chopped nuts and a small piece of edible silver leaf (if using).
6. Arrange the Sandesh on a serving plate or in a container lined with parchment paper.
7. Refrigerate the Sandesh for at least 1-2 hours to chill and firm up before serving.
8. Serve chilled Sandesh as a delightful dessert.

Enjoy the creamy and indulgent sweetness of homemade Sandesh, a quintessential Bengali delicacy!

Shutki

Ingredients:

- 100g Shutki (dried fish)
- 2 medium-sized onions, finely chopped
- 2-3 green chilies, finely chopped
- 2-3 garlic cloves, minced
- 1/2 teaspoon turmeric powder
- 1/2 teaspoon red chili powder (adjust to taste)
- Salt to taste
- Mustard oil for cooking
- Fresh coriander leaves for garnish (optional)

Instructions:

1. Begin by soaking the Shutki in warm water for about 30 minutes to soften it slightly. After soaking, drain the water and rinse the Shutki thoroughly to remove any excess salt.
2. In a pan, heat a tablespoon of mustard oil over medium heat. Add the drained Shutki to the pan and sauté for a few minutes until it becomes slightly crispy. Remove the Shutki from the pan and set aside.
3. In the same pan, add another tablespoon of mustard oil. Add the minced garlic and sauté until aromatic.
4. Add the chopped onions and green chilies to the pan. Sauté until the onions turn golden brown.
5. Reduce the heat to low and add the turmeric powder and red chili powder to the pan. Stir well to combine with the onions.
6. Return the fried Shutki to the pan. Mix well with the onion-spice mixture.
7. Using the back of a spoon or a potato masher, mash the Shutki along with the onions and spices until it forms a coarse paste.
8. Continue cooking the Shutki Bharta over low heat for another 5-7 minutes, stirring occasionally to prevent sticking.
9. Taste and adjust the seasoning, adding salt if necessary.
10. Once the Shutki Bharta is cooked through and the flavors have melded together, remove the pan from the heat.
11. Garnish the Shutki Bharta with fresh coriander leaves (if using).
12. Serve hot Shutki Bharta with steamed rice or your favorite bread.

Enjoy the robust and savory flavors of Shutki Bharta, a classic Bengali dish!

Jhal muri

Ingredients:

- 4 cups puffed rice (muri)
- 1 cup chopped cucumber
- 1 cup chopped tomatoes
- 1 cup chopped onions
- 1/2 cup roasted peanuts
- 1/4 cup chopped fresh coriander leaves
- 2 green chilies, finely chopped
- 2 tablespoons mustard oil
- 2 tablespoons tamarind chutney or date chutney
- 1 tablespoon mustard paste (optional)
- 1 tablespoon lemon juice
- 1 teaspoon roasted cumin powder
- 1 teaspoon chaat masala
- 1/2 teaspoon red chili powder (adjust to taste)
- Salt to taste
- Sev (fried gram flour vermicelli) for garnish
- Puffed rice (muri) for garnish

Instructions:

1. In a large mixing bowl, combine the puffed rice, chopped cucumber, tomatoes, onions, roasted peanuts, chopped coriander leaves, and green chilies.
2. In a small bowl, whisk together mustard oil, tamarind chutney or date chutney, mustard paste (if using), lemon juice, roasted cumin powder, chaat masala, red chili powder, and salt to taste.
3. Pour the dressing over the puffed rice and vegetable mixture. Toss well to coat everything evenly with the dressing.
4. Taste and adjust the seasoning if needed.
5. Garnish the Jhal Muri with a generous sprinkle of sev and additional puffed rice for extra crunch.
6. Serve the Jhal Muri immediately in bowls or paper cones.

Enjoy the spicy, tangy, and crunchy flavors of homemade Jhal Muri, a delightful street food snack from Bengal!

Roshogolla

Ingredients:

For the Rasgulla:

- 1 liter full-fat milk
- 2 tablespoons lemon juice or vinegar
- 1 cup sugar
- 4 cups water
- 1-2 tablespoons rose water or cardamom powder (optional)

Instructions:

1. Start by making the chhena (Indian cottage cheese). In a large pot, bring the milk to a gentle boil over medium heat.
2. Once the milk starts boiling, reduce the heat to low and add lemon juice or vinegar gradually, stirring continuously, until the milk curdles and separates into curds (chhena) and whey.
3. Line a colander with cheesecloth and pour the curdled milk into it. Rinse the chhena under cold water to remove the lemony taste.
4. Gather the corners of the cheesecloth and squeeze out any excess water from the chhena. Hang the cheesecloth for about 30 minutes to drain any remaining liquid.
5. Transfer the drained chhena to a large plate or bowl. Knead the chhena with the heel of your hand until it becomes smooth and soft. This will take about 7-10 minutes.
6. Divide the chhena dough into small portions and shape each portion into smooth balls. Make sure there are no cracks on the surface of the balls.
7. In a large pot, combine sugar and water. Bring the sugar syrup to a boil over medium heat, stirring occasionally to dissolve the sugar completely.
8. Gently drop the chhena balls into the boiling sugar syrup, one by one. Cover the pot with a lid and let the Rasgullas cook for about 15-20 minutes, or until they double in size and become soft and spongy.
9. If using rose water or cardamom powder, add it to the sugar syrup during the last few minutes of cooking.
10. Once the Rasgullas are cooked, turn off the heat and let them cool in the sugar syrup for a while.
11. Transfer the Rasgullas along with the sugar syrup to a serving bowl.
12. Serve the Rasgullas warm or chilled, as a delightful dessert.

Enjoy the soft and spongy goodness of homemade Rasgullas, a classic Bengali sweet treat!

Luchi

Ingredients:

- 2 cups refined flour (maida)
- 1/2 teaspoon salt
- Water, as needed
- Vegetable oil for deep-frying

Instructions:

1. In a mixing bowl, combine the refined flour and salt.
2. Gradually add water to the flour mixture and knead it into a soft, smooth dough. The dough should be pliable but not too sticky. Adjust the amount of water as needed.
3. Once the dough is formed, cover it with a damp cloth and let it rest for about 15-20 minutes.
4. After resting, divide the dough into small portions and shape each portion into a smooth ball.
5. Roll out each dough ball into a thin, round disc using a rolling pin. The thickness of the Luchi should be even throughout.
6. Heat vegetable oil in a deep frying pan or kadhai over medium heat.
7. Once the oil is hot, gently slide a rolled-out Luchi into the hot oil. Be careful not to overcrowd the pan.
8. Fry the Luchi on one side until it puffs up and turns golden brown. Then, flip it over and fry the other side until golden brown as well.
9. Once fried, remove the Luchi from the oil using a slotted spoon and drain excess oil by placing them on paper towels.
10. Repeat the process with the remaining dough balls, frying them in batches until all the Luchis are cooked.
11. Serve the hot and crispy Luchis immediately with your favorite curry or side dish.

Enjoy the delicious and fluffy Luchis as a delightful accompaniment to your Bengali meals!

Bhaji

Ingredients:

- Assorted vegetables (such as potatoes, onions, cauliflower, spinach, or eggplant), sliced or cut into bite-sized pieces
- 1 cup chickpea flour (besan)
- 2 tablespoons rice flour (optional, for extra crispiness)
- 1 teaspoon carom seeds (ajwain)
- 1 teaspoon turmeric powder
- 1 teaspoon red chili powder (adjust to taste)
- 1/2 teaspoon baking soda
- Salt to taste
- Water, as needed
- Vegetable oil for deep-frying

Instructions:

1. In a mixing bowl, combine chickpea flour, rice flour (if using), carom seeds, turmeric powder, red chili powder, baking soda, and salt.
2. Gradually add water to the flour mixture, whisking continuously, until you get a smooth and thick batter. The consistency should be similar to pancake batter, thick enough to coat the vegetables.
3. Heat vegetable oil in a deep frying pan or kadhai over medium heat.
4. Dip the sliced vegetables or vegetable pieces into the batter, ensuring they are well coated on all sides.
5. Gently slide the coated vegetables into the hot oil, one by one. Be careful not to overcrowd the pan.
6. Fry the Bhajis on medium heat until they turn golden brown and crispy on all sides. Flip them occasionally for even frying.
7. Once fried, remove the Bhajis from the oil using a slotted spoon and drain excess oil by placing them on paper towels.
8. Repeat the process with the remaining vegetables and batter, frying them in batches until all the Bhajis are cooked.
9. Serve the hot and crispy Bhajis immediately with green chutney or tamarind chutney.

Enjoy the delicious and flavorful Bhajis as a perfect snack for tea time or as an appetizer for gatherings!

Chotpoti

Ingredients:

- 1 cup dried yellow peas (soaked overnight)
- 1 large potato, diced
- 2 hard-boiled eggs, diced
- 1 onion, finely chopped
- 2 tomatoes, finely chopped
- 2 green chilies, finely chopped
- 2 tablespoons tamarind pulp
- 1 teaspoon red chili powder
- 1 teaspoon turmeric powder
- 1 teaspoon cumin powder
- 1 teaspoon coriander powder
- Salt to taste
- Oil for cooking
- Chopped cilantro and fried noodles or puffed rice for garnish
- Optional: yogurt for serving

Instructions:

1. Rinse the soaked yellow peas and boil them in a pot of water until they're soft and cooked through. Drain and set aside.
2. In another pot, boil the diced potatoes until they're tender. Drain and set aside.
3. In a large skillet, heat some oil over medium heat. Add the chopped onions and green chilies, and sauté until the onions turn translucent.
4. Add the chopped tomatoes to the skillet and cook until they soften.
5. Stir in the boiled yellow peas and diced potatoes.
6. Add the tamarind pulp, red chili powder, turmeric powder, cumin powder, coriander powder, and salt to the skillet. Mix well to combine all the ingredients.
7. Let the mixture simmer for a few minutes until the flavors meld together and the mixture thickens slightly.
8. Once cooked, remove the skillet from heat and transfer the Chotpoti to serving bowls.
9. Garnish each bowl with diced hard-boiled eggs, chopped cilantro, and fried noodles or puffed rice.
10. Serve the Chotpoti hot, optionally with a dollop of yogurt on top.

Feel free to adjust the spice levels and ingredients according to your taste preferences.

Enjoy your homemade Chotpoti!

Korma

Ingredients:

- 500g chicken, cut into bite-sized pieces
- 1 large onion, finely chopped
- 2 tomatoes, chopped
- 2 cloves garlic, minced
- 1-inch piece of ginger, grated
- 1/2 cup plain yogurt
- 1/4 cup heavy cream or coconut milk
- 2 tablespoons vegetable oil or ghee
- 1 teaspoon cumin seeds
- 2-3 green cardamom pods
- 2-3 cloves
- 1 cinnamon stick
- 1 bay leaf
- 1 teaspoon ground turmeric
- 1 teaspoon ground coriander
- 1 teaspoon garam masala
- 1/2 teaspoon ground cumin
- 1/2 teaspoon chili powder (adjust to taste)
- Salt to taste
- Chopped cilantro for garnish

Instructions:

1. Heat oil or ghee in a large skillet or pot over medium heat. Add the cumin seeds, cardamom pods, cloves, cinnamon stick, and bay leaf. Sauté for a minute until fragrant.
2. Add the chopped onions to the skillet and cook until they turn golden brown.
3. Stir in the minced garlic and grated ginger, and cook for another minute.
4. Add the chopped tomatoes to the skillet and cook until they soften and release their juices.
5. Add the ground turmeric, ground coriander, ground cumin, chili powder, and salt to the skillet. Mix well to combine with the onion-tomato mixture.
6. Add the chicken pieces to the skillet and coat them evenly with the spice mixture.
7. Reduce the heat to low and add the plain yogurt to the skillet. Stir well to combine.

8. Cover the skillet and let the chicken cook for about 15-20 minutes, stirring occasionally, until the chicken is cooked through and tender.
9. Once the chicken is cooked, stir in the heavy cream or coconut milk and garam masala. Simmer for another 5 minutes.
10. Adjust the seasoning if needed and remove the skillet from heat.
11. Garnish the Chicken Korma with chopped cilantro and serve hot with rice, naan, or roti.

Enjoy your homemade Chicken Korma!

Piyaju

Ingredients:

- 1 cup yellow split peas (soaked for 3-4 hours)
- 1 onion, finely chopped
- 2-3 green chilies, finely chopped (adjust to taste)
- 2 tablespoons chopped cilantro
- 1 teaspoon ginger paste
- 1 teaspoon garlic paste
- 1 teaspoon cumin seeds
- 1/2 teaspoon turmeric powder
- Salt to taste
- Vegetable oil for frying

Instructions:

1. Drain the soaked split peas and rinse them thoroughly.
2. In a food processor or blender, grind the split peas into a coarse paste. You may need to add a little water to facilitate the grinding process, but be careful not to make the mixture too watery.
3. Transfer the ground split peas to a mixing bowl and add the chopped onions, green chilies, cilantro, ginger paste, garlic paste, cumin seeds, turmeric powder, and salt. Mix well to combine all the ingredients.
4. Heat vegetable oil in a deep frying pan or pot over medium heat.
5. Take a small portion of the mixture in your hand and shape it into a small round patty or fritter.
6. Carefully slide the fritter into the hot oil and fry until it turns golden brown and crispy on both sides. Fry the fritters in batches, making sure not to overcrowd the pan.
7. Once the fritters are cooked, remove them from the oil using a slotted spoon and drain them on paper towels to remove excess oil.
8. Repeat the frying process with the remaining mixture until all the fritters are cooked.
9. Serve the Piyaju hot with your favorite dipping sauce or chutney.

Enjoy your crispy and flavorful Piyaju as a delicious snack or appetizer!

Bhapa chingri

Ingredients:

- 500g large prawns (cleaned and deveined)
- 2 tablespoons mustard paste
- 2 tablespoons coconut paste
- 2 tablespoons yogurt
- 1 teaspoon ginger paste
- 1 teaspoon garlic paste
- 1 teaspoon turmeric powder
- 1 teaspoon red chili powder (adjust to taste)
- Salt to taste
- Mustard oil for cooking
- Fresh cilantro leaves for garnish
- Sliced green chilies for garnish

Instructions:

1. In a mixing bowl, combine the mustard paste, coconut paste, yogurt, ginger paste, garlic paste, turmeric powder, red chili powder, and salt. Mix well to form a smooth marinade.
2. Add the cleaned prawns to the marinade and coat them evenly with the mixture. Make sure the prawns are well coated. Allow them to marinate for at least 30 minutes to an hour in the refrigerator.
3. Prepare a steamer by bringing water to a boil in the bottom part of the steamer.
4. While the water is heating, prepare a shallow dish or plate by greasing it lightly with mustard oil.
5. Arrange the marinated prawns in the greased dish in a single layer.
6. Once the water in the steamer is boiling, carefully place the dish with the prawns inside the steamer. Cover and steam the prawns for about 15-20 minutes, or until they are cooked through.
7. After steaming, remove the dish from the steamer and let it cool slightly.
8. Drizzle a little mustard oil over the steamed prawns for extra flavor.
9. Garnish with fresh cilantro leaves and sliced green chilies.
10. Serve the Bhapa Chingri hot with steamed rice or as part of a traditional Bengali meal.

Enjoy the tender and flavorful Bhapa Chingri as a delightful seafood dish!

Shobji bhorta

Ingredients:

- 2 cups mixed vegetables (such as potatoes, carrots, green peas, cauliflower, green beans, etc.), boiled and mashed
- 1 onion, finely chopped
- 2-3 green chilies, finely chopped (adjust to taste)
- 2 cloves garlic, minced
- 1-inch piece of ginger, grated
- 2 tablespoons mustard oil
- 1 teaspoon panch phoron (a Bengali spice mix of equal parts cumin seeds, fennel seeds, fenugreek seeds, mustard seeds, and nigella seeds)
- 1/2 teaspoon turmeric powder
- Salt to taste
- Fresh cilantro leaves for garnish (optional)

Instructions:

1. Heat mustard oil in a pan over medium heat.
2. Add the panch phoron to the hot oil and let it splutter for a few seconds, releasing its aromatic flavors.
3. Add the chopped onion to the pan and sauté until it turns golden brown.
4. Add the minced garlic, grated ginger, and chopped green chilies to the pan. Sauté for another minute until the raw aroma disappears.
5. Add the turmeric powder to the pan and mix well with the onion-garlic-ginger mixture.
6. Add the mashed mixed vegetables to the pan and mix thoroughly with the onion-spice mixture.
7. Cook the mixture for a few minutes, stirring occasionally, until the flavors are well combined and the vegetables are heated through.
8. Season with salt to taste and mix well.
9. Once cooked, remove the pan from heat and transfer the Shobji Bhorta to a serving dish.
10. Garnish with fresh cilantro leaves, if desired.
11. Serve hot as a side dish with rice, bread, or any main course of your choice.

Enjoy the comforting and flavorful Shobji Bhorta as a delicious addition to your meal!

Prawn curry

Ingredients:

- 500g prawns, peeled and deveined
- 2 tablespoons vegetable oil
- 1 onion, finely chopped
- 2 tomatoes, chopped
- 2 green chilies, slit lengthwise
- 1 teaspoon ginger paste
- 1 teaspoon garlic paste
- 1 teaspoon ground turmeric
- 1 teaspoon ground cumin
- 1 teaspoon ground coriander
- 1/2 teaspoon chili powder (adjust to taste)
- 1 teaspoon garam masala
- Salt to taste
- 1 cup coconut milk (optional)
- Fresh cilantro leaves for garnish

Instructions:

1. Heat the vegetable oil in a large pan over medium heat.
2. Add the chopped onion to the pan and sauté until it becomes soft and translucent.
3. Add the ginger paste and garlic paste to the pan and sauté for another minute until the raw aroma disappears.
4. Add the chopped tomatoes and green chilies to the pan and cook until the tomatoes soften and release their juices.
5. Stir in the ground turmeric, ground cumin, ground coriander, chili powder, and salt. Cook the spices for a minute until they are fragrant.
6. Add the prawns to the pan and stir well to coat them with the spice mixture.
7. If using coconut milk, pour it into the pan and mix well with the prawns and spices.
8. Cover the pan and let the prawns simmer in the curry sauce for about 5-7 minutes, or until they are cooked through. Be careful not to overcook the prawns as they can become tough.

9. Once the prawns are cooked, sprinkle garam masala over the curry and give it a final stir.
10. Remove the pan from heat and garnish the prawn curry with fresh cilantro leaves.
11. Serve hot with steamed rice or naan bread.

Enjoy your delicious prawn curry packed with flavor and aroma!

Doi maach

Ingredients:

- 500g fish fillets (such as Rohu, Katla, or any firm-fleshed fish)
- 1 cup plain yogurt (preferably whole milk)
- 1 onion, finely chopped
- 2 tomatoes, chopped
- 2 green chilies, slit lengthwise
- 1 teaspoon ginger paste
- 1 teaspoon garlic paste
- 1 teaspoon ground turmeric
- 1 teaspoon ground cumin
- 1 teaspoon ground coriander
- 1/2 teaspoon chili powder (adjust to taste)
- 1 teaspoon sugar
- Salt to taste
- 2 tablespoons vegetable oil
- Fresh cilantro leaves for garnish

Instructions:

1. Wash the fish fillets thoroughly and pat them dry with paper towels. Cut them into pieces if they are too large.
2. In a bowl, whisk the plain yogurt until smooth. Set aside.
3. Heat vegetable oil in a large pan over medium heat.
4. Add the chopped onion to the pan and sauté until it becomes soft and translucent.
5. Add the ginger paste and garlic paste to the pan and sauté for another minute until the raw aroma disappears.
6. Add the chopped tomatoes and green chilies to the pan and cook until the tomatoes soften and release their juices.
7. Stir in the ground turmeric, ground cumin, ground coriander, chili powder, sugar, and salt. Cook the spices for a minute until they are fragrant.
8. Reduce the heat to low and slowly pour the whisked yogurt into the pan, stirring continuously to prevent it from curdling.
9. Once the yogurt is incorporated into the spice mixture, add the fish pieces to the pan and gently coat them with the gravy.

10. Cover the pan and let the fish simmer in the yogurt gravy for about 10-15 minutes, or until the fish is cooked through and the gravy thickens.
11. Once the fish is cooked, garnish the Doi Maach with fresh cilantro leaves.
12. Serve hot with steamed rice or roti.

Enjoy your creamy and flavorful Doi Maach!

Shingara

Ingredients:

For the filling:

- 2 large potatoes, boiled, peeled, and mashed
- 1/2 cup green peas, boiled
- 1 onion, finely chopped
- 2 green chilies, finely chopped (adjust to taste)
- 1 teaspoon ginger paste
- 1 teaspoon garlic paste
- 1 teaspoon cumin seeds
- 1 teaspoon coriander powder
- 1/2 teaspoon turmeric powder
- 1/2 teaspoon garam masala
- 1 tablespoon vegetable oil
- Salt to taste
- Chopped cilantro leaves for garnish

For the dough:

- 2 cups all-purpose flour
- 2 tablespoons vegetable oil or ghee
- 1/2 teaspoon salt
- Water, as needed

Instructions:

1. Start by preparing the filling. Heat vegetable oil in a pan over medium heat.
2. Add the cumin seeds to the hot oil and let them splutter for a few seconds.
3. Add the chopped onion to the pan and sauté until it becomes soft and translucent.
4. Add the ginger paste and garlic paste to the pan and sauté for another minute until the raw aroma disappears.
5. Add the mashed potatoes, boiled peas, chopped green chilies, coriander powder, turmeric powder, garam masala, and salt to the pan. Mix well to combine all the

ingredients. Cook for a few minutes until the filling is heated through and well combined. Remove from heat and set aside to cool.
6. To make the dough, sift the all-purpose flour into a mixing bowl. Add salt and vegetable oil or ghee. Rub the oil into the flour until it resembles breadcrumbs.
7. Gradually add water, a little at a time, and knead the dough until it's smooth and pliable. Cover the dough with a damp cloth and let it rest for about 20-30 minutes.
8. After the resting period, divide the dough into small equal-sized balls.
9. Roll out each ball into a thin circle using a rolling pin.
10. Cut each circle in half to form semi-circles.
11. Take one semi-circle and fold it into a cone shape, sealing the edges with water.
12. Place a spoonful of the prepared filling into the cone.
13. Fold the open edge of the cone to seal it, forming a triangular shape. Press the edges to ensure they are sealed.
14. Repeat the process with the remaining dough and filling.
15. Heat vegetable oil in a deep frying pan over medium heat.
16. Once the oil is hot, carefully add the prepared Shingaras in batches and fry them until they turn golden brown and crispy on all sides.
17. Remove the fried Shingaras using a slotted spoon and drain them on paper towels to remove excess oil.
18. Serve the Shingaras hot with your favorite dipping sauce or chutney.

Enjoy your homemade Shingaras as a delicious snack or appetizer!

Borhani

Ingredients:

- 2 cups plain yogurt
- 2 cups cold water
- 1/2 teaspoon roasted cumin powder
- 1/2 teaspoon ground black pepper
- 1/2 teaspoon ground ginger
- 1/2 teaspoon ground coriander
- 1/2 teaspoon ground mint (optional)
- 1 tablespoon chopped fresh cilantro leaves
- 1 tablespoon chopped fresh mint leaves
- 1 tablespoon chopped fresh green chilies (adjust to taste)
- Salt to taste
- Sugar to taste (optional)
- Ice cubes for serving
- Fresh mint leaves and sliced cucumber for garnish (optional)

Instructions:

1. In a large bowl, whisk together the plain yogurt and cold water until smooth and well combined.
2. Add the roasted cumin powder, ground black pepper, ground ginger, ground coriander, and ground mint (if using) to the yogurt mixture. Mix well.
3. Add the chopped cilantro leaves, chopped mint leaves, and chopped green chilies to the bowl. Stir to combine.
4. Taste the Borhani and adjust the seasoning by adding salt and sugar to taste, if desired. Mix well until the salt and sugar are dissolved.
5. Chill the Borhani in the refrigerator for at least 1-2 hours before serving to allow the flavors to meld together.
6. Just before serving, add some ice cubes to the Borhani to keep it cold.
7. Pour the chilled Borhani into serving glasses.
8. Garnish each glass with a sprig of fresh mint leaves and a slice of cucumber, if desired.
9. Serve immediately as a refreshing drink alongside spicy dishes or as a welcome drink during special occasions.

Enjoy the cool and tangy flavors of Borhani as a delightful accompaniment to your meals!

Khichuri

Ingredients:

- 1 cup rice (any variety like basmati or parboiled rice)
- 1/2 cup yellow lentils (moong dal)
- 1 onion, thinly sliced
- 1 potato, diced
- 1 carrot, diced
- 1/2 cup green peas (fresh or frozen)
- 2-3 green chilies, slit lengthwise (adjust to taste)
- 1 teaspoon ginger paste
- 1 teaspoon garlic paste
- 1 teaspoon cumin seeds
- 1 cinnamon stick
- 2-3 green cardamom pods
- 2-3 cloves
- 1 bay leaf
- 1/2 teaspoon turmeric powder
- 1/2 teaspoon ground cumin
- 1/2 teaspoon ground coriander
- Salt to taste
- Vegetable oil or ghee for cooking
- Fresh cilantro leaves for garnish
- Lemon wedges for serving (optional)

Instructions:

1. Rinse the rice and lentils separately under running water until the water runs clear. Drain and set aside.
2. Heat some vegetable oil or ghee in a large pot over medium heat.
3. Add the cumin seeds, cinnamon stick, cardamom pods, cloves, and bay leaf to the hot oil. Sauté for a minute until the spices become fragrant.
4. Add the thinly sliced onion to the pot and sauté until it turns golden brown.
5. Stir in the ginger paste and garlic paste, and sauté for another minute.
6. Add the diced potato, carrot, and green peas to the pot. Sauté for a few minutes until the vegetables are lightly browned.

7. Add the drained rice and lentils to the pot. Mix well with the vegetables and spices.
8. Add turmeric powder, ground cumin, ground coriander, and salt to taste. Mix everything together.
9. Pour enough water into the pot to cover the rice and lentils by about an inch.
10. Bring the mixture to a boil, then reduce the heat to low. Cover the pot and let the Khichuri simmer gently for about 20-25 minutes, or until the rice and lentils are cooked through and the mixture has thickened to your desired consistency.
11. Once cooked, remove the pot from heat and let it sit for a few minutes.
12. Garnish the Khichuri with fresh cilantro leaves.
13. Serve hot with a side of lemon wedges, if desired.

Enjoy your comforting and flavorful Khichuri as a wholesome meal! You can also serve it with fried eggplant slices, papadum, or any pickle for added flavor.

Beef rezala

Ingredients:

- 500g beef, cut into bite-sized pieces
- 1 cup plain yogurt
- 1 onion, finely chopped
- 2 tablespoons ginger paste
- 2 tablespoons garlic paste
- 1/2 cup cashew nuts, soaked in water for 30 minutes
- 1/4 cup poppy seeds, soaked in water for 30 minutes
- 1/4 cup desiccated coconut
- 1 teaspoon white peppercorns
- 4-5 green cardamom pods
- 2-3 cloves
- 1-inch piece of cinnamon stick
- 2 bay leaves
- 2 tablespoons vegetable oil or ghee
- 1/2 cup heavy cream
- Salt to taste
- Sugar to taste
- Chopped cilantro leaves for garnish

Instructions:

1. In a blender or food processor, combine the soaked cashew nuts, soaked poppy seeds, desiccated coconut, white peppercorns, green cardamom pods, cloves, cinnamon stick, and a little water. Blend into a smooth paste. Set aside.
2. In a mixing bowl, whisk the plain yogurt until smooth. Add the ginger paste, garlic paste, and a pinch of salt. Mix well.
3. Marinate the beef pieces in the yogurt mixture, making sure they are well coated. Cover and refrigerate for at least 1 hour, or preferably overnight.
4. Heat vegetable oil or ghee in a large pot or Dutch oven over medium heat.
5. Add the chopped onion to the pot and sauté until it turns golden brown.
6. Add the marinated beef to the pot along with any excess marinade. Cook, stirring occasionally, until the beef is browned on all sides.
7. Add the prepared spice paste to the pot and mix well with the beef.

8. Pour in enough water to cover the beef, about 1-2 cups depending on the desired consistency of the gravy.
9. Add the bay leaves to the pot and season with salt and sugar to taste. Mix well.
10. Cover the pot and let the beef simmer over low heat for about 1-2 hours, or until the beef is tender and the gravy has thickened.
11. Once the beef is cooked, stir in the heavy cream and let it simmer for another 5-10 minutes.
12. Adjust the seasoning if needed.
13. Remove the pot from heat and garnish the Beef Rezala with chopped cilantro leaves.
14. Serve hot with steamed rice, naan, or paratha.

Enjoy the rich and flavorful Beef Rezala as a special dish for any occasion!

Piyajoo pitha

Ingredients:

- 1 cup yellow lentils (moong dal), soaked for 3-4 hours
- 1 large onion, finely chopped
- 2-3 green chilies, finely chopped (adjust to taste)
- 2 tablespoons chopped fresh cilantro leaves
- 1 teaspoon ginger paste
- 1 teaspoon garlic paste
- 1 teaspoon cumin seeds
- 1/2 teaspoon turmeric powder
- Salt to taste
- Vegetable oil for deep frying

Instructions:

1. Rinse the soaked lentils and drain them well.
2. In a blender or food processor, grind the lentils into a coarse paste without adding any water. Transfer the ground lentils to a mixing bowl.
3. Add the finely chopped onion, green chilies, chopped cilantro leaves, ginger paste, garlic paste, cumin seeds, turmeric powder, and salt to the bowl with the ground lentils. Mix well to combine all the ingredients thoroughly.
4. Heat vegetable oil in a deep frying pan or wok over medium heat.
5. Once the oil is hot, take small portions of the lentil mixture in your hand and shape them into small round patties or fritters.
6. Carefully slide the fritters into the hot oil, making sure not to overcrowd the pan.
7. Fry the fritters in batches until they turn golden brown and crispy on all sides, turning them occasionally with a slotted spoon for even cooking.
8. Once the fritters are cooked, remove them from the oil using a slotted spoon and drain them on paper towels to remove excess oil.
9. Repeat the frying process with the remaining lentil mixture until all the fritters are cooked.
10. Serve the Piyaju Pitha hot with your favorite dipping sauce or chutney.

Enjoy the crispy and flavorful Piyaju Pitha as a delicious snack or appetizer!

Malai curry

Ingredients:

- 500g boneless chicken, cut into bite-sized pieces (you can also use prawns, fish, or paneer for vegetarian option)
- 1 onion, finely chopped
- 2 tomatoes, chopped
- 1 cup coconut milk
- 2 tablespoons vegetable oil or ghee
- 1 teaspoon ginger paste
- 1 teaspoon garlic paste
- 1 teaspoon ground turmeric
- 1 teaspoon ground cumin
- 1 teaspoon ground coriander
- 1/2 teaspoon chili powder (adjust to taste)
- 1/2 teaspoon garam masala
- Salt to taste
- Fresh cilantro leaves for garnish

Instructions:

1. Heat vegetable oil or ghee in a large pan over medium heat.
2. Add the chopped onion to the pan and sauté until it turns golden brown.
3. Add the ginger paste and garlic paste to the pan and sauté for another minute until the raw aroma disappears.
4. Add the chopped tomatoes to the pan and cook until they soften and release their juices.
5. Stir in the ground turmeric, ground cumin, ground coriander, chili powder, and salt. Cook the spices for a minute until they are fragrant.
6. Add the chicken pieces to the pan and coat them evenly with the spice mixture. If using seafood or paneer, you can skip this step and directly add them later.
7. Pour in the coconut milk and mix well with the chicken and spices.
8. Cover the pan and let the curry simmer over low heat for about 15-20 minutes, or until the chicken is cooked through and tender. If using seafood or paneer, add them to the curry during the last 5-10 minutes of cooking and cook until they are cooked through.

9. Once the chicken is cooked, sprinkle garam masala over the curry and give it a final stir.
10. Remove the pan from heat and garnish the Malai Curry with fresh cilantro leaves.
11. Serve hot with steamed rice or naan bread.

Enjoy the creamy and flavorful Malai Curry as a delightful addition to your meal!

Pati shapta

Ingredients:

For the pancake batter:

- 1 cup all-purpose flour
- 1/2 cup rice flour
- 2 cups milk
- 1/4 cup water
- 2 tablespoons sugar
- 1/4 teaspoon salt
- Vegetable oil or ghee for cooking

For the filling:

- 1 cup grated coconut (fresh or frozen)
- 1/2 cup khoya (milk solids)
- 1/2 cup jaggery (or sugar)
- 1/2 teaspoon ground cardamom
- Chopped nuts (such as almonds, cashews, or pistachios) for garnish (optional)

Instructions:

1. To make the filling, heat a pan over medium heat and add the grated coconut, khoya, and jaggery (or sugar). Cook, stirring continuously, until the mixture thickens and the jaggery melts. Add the ground cardamom and mix well. Remove from heat and set aside to cool.
2. To make the pancake batter, sift together the all-purpose flour and rice flour into a mixing bowl. Add sugar and salt, and mix well.
3. Gradually add milk and water to the flour mixture, whisking continuously to form a smooth batter without any lumps. The consistency of the batter should be similar to that of crepe batter.
4. Heat a non-stick pan or griddle over medium heat. Lightly grease the pan with vegetable oil or ghee.

5. Pour a ladleful of batter onto the pan and spread it thinly into a round shape using the back of the ladle. Cook for about 1-2 minutes, or until the edges start to lift and the bottom is lightly golden.
6. Spoon some of the coconut and khoya filling onto one side of the pancake. Fold the other side over the filling to form a half-moon shape.
7. Gently press down on the edges to seal the pancake. Cook for another 1-2 minutes, or until the pancake is cooked through and golden brown on both sides.
8. Repeat the process with the remaining batter and filling.
9. Once all the Pati Shaptas are cooked, transfer them to a serving plate and garnish with chopped nuts, if desired.
10. Serve warm or at room temperature as a delicious dessert.

Enjoy your homemade Pati Shapta, filled with the sweet and aromatic flavors of coconut and khoya!

Chanar payesh

Ingredients:

- 1 liter full-fat milk
- 1 lemon (for making chhana)
- 1/2 cup sugar (adjust to taste)
- 4-5 green cardamom pods, crushed
- 2 tablespoons chopped nuts (such as almonds, cashews, or pistachios)
- 1 tablespoon raisins (optional)
- A pinch of saffron strands (optional)
- Rose water or kewra water for flavoring (optional)

Instructions:

1. Start by making chhana (paneer). Heat the milk in a large pot over medium heat until it comes to a gentle boil. Once it starts boiling, reduce the heat to low.
2. Cut the lemon in half and squeeze the juice into the milk. Stir gently until the milk curdles and the whey separates from the curds.
3. Line a strainer or colander with a muslin cloth or cheesecloth. Pour the curdled milk into the cloth to collect the chhana. Rinse the chhana under cold water to remove the lemony flavor.
4. Gather the edges of the cloth and squeeze out any excess liquid from the chhana. Hang the cloth for 30 minutes to drain excess whey.
5. After 30 minutes, transfer the chhana to a clean plate and knead it with your hands until smooth and creamy. This process helps to remove any remaining moisture.
6. In a separate pot, heat the milk over medium heat. Let it simmer, stirring occasionally, until it reduces to about three-fourths of its original volume.
7. Add the sugar to the milk and stir until dissolved. Continue to simmer for a few more minutes until the milk thickens slightly.
8. Crumble the chhana into the simmering milk, stirring gently to incorporate it evenly.
9. Add the crushed cardamom pods, chopped nuts, and raisins (if using) to the pot. Stir well to combine.
10. If using saffron strands, soak them in a tablespoon of warm milk for a few minutes, then add them to the pot along with the milk.

11. Continue to simmer the mixture for another 5-10 minutes, stirring occasionally, until the flavors meld together and the payesh thickens to your desired consistency.
12. Once done, remove the pot from heat and let the Chanar Payesh cool slightly.
13. Add a few drops of rose water or kewra water for flavoring, if desired.
14. Transfer the Chanar Payesh to serving bowls or glasses. Garnish with additional chopped nuts and saffron strands, if desired.
15. Serve warm or chilled, as per your preference.

Enjoy the creamy and flavorful Chanar Payesh as a delightful dessert after your meal!

Chicken rezala

Ingredients:

For marinating the chicken:

- 500g boneless chicken, cut into bite-sized pieces
- 1 cup plain yogurt
- 1 tablespoon ginger paste
- 1 tablespoon garlic paste
- 1/2 teaspoon ground white pepper
- 1/2 teaspoon ground cardamom
- Salt to taste

For the gravy:

- 2 tablespoons vegetable oil or ghee
- 1 onion, finely chopped
- 1 teaspoon ginger paste
- 1 teaspoon garlic paste
- 1 teaspoon ground white pepper
- 1 teaspoon ground cardamom
- 1/2 teaspoon ground nutmeg
- 1/2 teaspoon ground mace
- 1/2 teaspoon ground cinnamon
- 1/2 teaspoon ground cloves
- 1 cup plain yogurt
- 1/2 cup heavy cream
- Salt to taste
- Sugar to taste
- Chopped fresh cilantro leaves for garnish

Instructions:

1. In a mixing bowl, combine the plain yogurt, ginger paste, garlic paste, ground white pepper, ground cardamom, and salt. Mix well to form a smooth marinade.

2. Add the chicken pieces to the marinade and coat them evenly. Cover and refrigerate for at least 1 hour, or preferably overnight, to allow the flavors to meld.
3. Heat vegetable oil or ghee in a large pan over medium heat.
4. Add the chopped onion to the pan and sauté until it turns golden brown.
5. Add the ginger paste and garlic paste to the pan and sauté for another minute until the raw aroma disappears.
6. Add the marinated chicken to the pan, along with any excess marinade. Cook, stirring occasionally, until the chicken is lightly browned on all sides.
7. In a small bowl, whisk together the plain yogurt and heavy cream until smooth.
8. Add the ground white pepper, ground cardamom, ground nutmeg, ground mace, ground cinnamon, and ground cloves to the pan. Mix well with the chicken.
9. Pour the yogurt and cream mixture into the pan, stirring continuously to combine with the chicken and spices.
10. Lower the heat and let the chicken simmer gently in the gravy for about 15-20 minutes, or until the chicken is cooked through and the gravy thickens.
11. Adjust the seasoning with salt and sugar to taste.
12. Once the chicken is cooked and the gravy reaches your desired consistency, remove the pan from heat.
13. Garnish the Chicken Rezala with chopped fresh cilantro leaves.
14. Serve hot with steamed rice, pulao, or naan bread.

Enjoy the rich and aromatic Chicken Rezala as a delightful main course!

Dhokar dalna

Ingredients:

For making the lentil cakes (dhoka):

- 1 cup chana dal (split Bengal gram)
- 2-3 green chilies, chopped
- 1 teaspoon ginger paste
- 1 teaspoon cumin seeds
- 1 teaspoon turmeric powder
- Salt to taste
- Vegetable oil for frying

For the gravy:

- 2 tablespoons vegetable oil
- 1 onion, finely chopped
- 2 tomatoes, chopped
- 1 teaspoon ginger paste
- 1 teaspoon garlic paste
- 1 teaspoon cumin seeds
- 1 teaspoon turmeric powder
- 1 teaspoon ground coriander
- 1 teaspoon red chili powder (adjust to taste)
- 1/2 teaspoon garam masala
- Salt to taste
- Fresh cilantro leaves for garnish

Instructions:

1. Rinse the chana dal thoroughly and soak it in water for at least 4-5 hours or overnight.
2. Drain the soaked dal and transfer it to a blender or food processor. Add the chopped green chilies, ginger paste, cumin seeds, turmeric powder, and salt. Blend into a coarse paste without adding any water.

3. Heat vegetable oil in a non-stick pan over medium heat. Once the oil is hot, add the lentil paste to the pan and spread it evenly to form a thick layer. Cook for about 8-10 minutes or until the bottom is golden brown and crispy.
4. Flip the lentil cake and cook the other side until it's golden brown and crispy as well. Remove from the pan and let it cool slightly.
5. Once cooled, cut the lentil cake into diamond-shaped pieces or any desired shape.
6. Heat vegetable oil in a deep frying pan or kadhai over medium heat. Fry the lentil cake pieces until they turn golden brown and crispy. Remove from oil and set aside.
7. In the same pan, heat 2 tablespoons of vegetable oil. Add the cumin seeds and let them splutter.
8. Add the finely chopped onion to the pan and sauté until it turns golden brown.
9. Add the ginger paste and garlic paste to the pan. Sauté for another minute until the raw aroma disappears.
10. Add the chopped tomatoes to the pan and cook until they soften and release their juices.
11. Stir in the turmeric powder, ground coriander, red chili powder, and salt. Cook the spices for a minute until they are fragrant.
12. Add 1-2 cups of water to the pan to make the gravy. Bring it to a simmer.
13. Gently add the fried lentil cake pieces (dhoka) to the gravy. Cover and let it simmer for about 8-10 minutes to allow the flavors to meld together and the lentil cakes to soak up the gravy.
14. Sprinkle garam masala over the Dhokar Dalna and give it a final stir.
15. Garnish with fresh cilantro leaves and serve hot with steamed rice or luchi (deep-fried flatbread).

Enjoy the delicious and aromatic Dhokar Dalna as a flavorful Bengali delicacy!

Jorda pulao

Ingredients:

- 1 cup basmati rice
- 2 cups water
- 1/4 cup sugar (adjust to taste)
- A pinch of saffron strands
- 2-3 tablespoons milk
- 2-3 tablespoons ghee (clarified butter)
- 2-3 green cardamom pods
- 1-inch piece of cinnamon stick
- 4-5 cloves
- 1/4 cup mixed nuts (such as almonds, cashews, and raisins)
- A few drops of rose water (optional)
- Edible food color (optional, for vibrant colors)

Instructions:

1. Rinse the basmati rice under cold water until the water runs clear. Soak the rice in water for about 30 minutes. Drain and set aside.
2. In a small bowl, soak the saffron strands in warm milk. Set aside for about 15-20 minutes to let the saffron infuse the milk with its color and aroma.
3. In a large pot, bring 2 cups of water to a boil. Add the soaked and drained rice to the boiling water. Cook the rice until it's about 70-80% done. Drain the rice and set it aside.
4. In a separate pan, heat ghee over medium heat. Add the green cardamom pods, cinnamon stick, and cloves to the ghee. Sauté for a minute until the spices become fragrant.
5. Add the mixed nuts to the pan and sauté until they turn golden brown. Add the raisins and sauté until they plump up.
6. Add the cooked rice to the pan with the spices and nuts. Gently mix everything together.
7. Sprinkle sugar over the rice and mix well. Allow the sugar to melt and caramelize slightly.
8. Pour the saffron-infused milk over the rice. Add a few drops of rose water for extra fragrance, if using.
9. If desired, divide the rice into portions and mix each portion with a different food color to create vibrant layers.

10. Cover the pan with a lid and let the Jorda Pulao simmer over low heat for about 10-15 minutes to allow the flavors to meld together and for the rice to finish cooking.
11. Once done, gently fluff the rice with a fork.
12. Transfer the Jorda Pulao to a serving platter and garnish with additional nuts and saffron strands if desired.
13. Serve hot as a festive and aromatic rice dish.

Enjoy the delightful flavors and colors of Jorda Pulao as a special treat for your celebrations!

Kathal curry

Ingredients:

- 500g young jackfruit (kathal), peeled and chopped into bite-sized pieces
- 2 onions, finely chopped
- 2 tomatoes, finely chopped
- 2-3 green chilies, slit lengthwise (adjust to taste)
- 1 tablespoon ginger-garlic paste
- 1 teaspoon cumin seeds
- 1 teaspoon mustard seeds
- 1 teaspoon turmeric powder
- 1 teaspoon ground coriander
- 1/2 teaspoon red chili powder (adjust to taste)
- 1/2 teaspoon garam masala
- 1/2 teaspoon ground fennel seeds
- Salt to taste
- Vegetable oil for cooking
- Fresh cilantro leaves for garnish

Instructions:

1. Heat vegetable oil in a large pan or pot over medium heat. Add the cumin seeds and mustard seeds and let them splutter.
2. Add the finely chopped onions to the pan and sauté until they turn golden brown.
3. Add the ginger-garlic paste to the pan and sauté for another minute until the raw aroma disappears.
4. Add the chopped tomatoes to the pan and cook until they turn soft and mushy.
5. Stir in the turmeric powder, ground coriander, red chili powder, and ground fennel seeds. Mix well to combine the spices with the onion-tomato mixture.
6. Add the chopped jackfruit pieces to the pan and mix well with the spice mixture.
7. Pour in enough water to cover the jackfruit pieces. Season with salt to taste.
8. Cover the pan and let the jackfruit curry simmer over low heat for about 20-25 minutes, or until the jackfruit is tender and cooked through. Stir occasionally and add more water if needed to prevent the curry from drying out.
9. Once the jackfruit is cooked, sprinkle garam masala over the curry and give it a final stir.

10. Remove the pan from heat and garnish the Kathal Curry with fresh cilantro leaves.
11. Serve hot with steamed rice, roti, or naan bread.

Enjoy the flavorful and aromatic Kathal Curry as a delightful vegetarian dish!

Kochu shak

Ingredients:

- 1 bunch of taro leaves (kochu shak), cleaned and chopped
- 1 medium-sized potato, peeled and diced
- 1 onion, finely chopped
- 2-3 green chilies, slit lengthwise (adjust to taste)
- 1 tablespoon mustard oil or vegetable oil
- 1 teaspoon mustard seeds
- 1 teaspoon cumin seeds
- 1 teaspoon turmeric powder
- 1/2 teaspoon red chili powder (adjust to taste)
- Salt to taste
- Water, as needed
- Fresh cilantro leaves for garnish (optional)

Instructions:

1. Heat mustard oil or vegetable oil in a large pan or pot over medium heat.
2. Add the mustard seeds and cumin seeds to the hot oil. Let them splutter.
3. Add the finely chopped onion to the pan and sauté until it turns golden brown.
4. Add the diced potato to the pan and cook for a few minutes until it starts to soften.
5. Stir in the turmeric powder and red chili powder. Mix well to coat the potatoes with the spices.
6. Add the chopped taro leaves to the pan. Mix well with the potatoes and onions.
7. Season with salt to taste. Add the slit green chilies to the pan for added flavor and heat.
8. Pour in enough water to cover the taro leaves and potatoes. Cover the pan and let the mixture simmer over low heat for about 15-20 minutes, or until the taro leaves and potatoes are cooked through and tender.
9. Once the vegetables are cooked, remove the pan from heat.
10. Garnish the Kochu Shak with fresh cilantro leaves, if desired.
11. Serve hot with steamed rice or roti.

Enjoy the nutritious and flavorful Kochu Shak as a comforting and wholesome Bengali dish!

Lalmohon

Ingredients:

For the dough:

- 2 cups grated coconut (fresh or desiccated)
- 1 cup sugar
- 1/2 cup rice flour (optional, for binding)
- Water, as needed

For the sugar syrup:

- 1 cup sugar
- 1 cup water
- 2-3 cardamom pods, crushed (or a few drops of rose water for flavor)

Instructions:

1. In a mixing bowl, combine the grated coconut and sugar. If using rice flour, add it to the mixture as well. Mix well until everything is evenly combined.
2. Gradually add water to the mixture, a little at a time, and knead to form a smooth dough. The consistency should be firm enough to hold its shape when formed into balls or patties.
3. Take small portions of the dough and shape them into small balls or patties. Press them gently to flatten slightly.
4. Heat vegetable oil in a deep frying pan or kadhai over medium heat.
5. Once the oil is hot, carefully add the shaped dough pieces to the hot oil in batches. Fry them until they turn golden brown and crispy on all sides.
6. Remove the fried Lalmohon from the oil using a slotted spoon and drain them on paper towels to remove excess oil.
7. In a separate saucepan, combine sugar and water to make the sugar syrup. Add crushed cardamom pods or rose water for flavor, if desired.
8. Bring the sugar syrup to a boil and then reduce the heat to simmer. Let it simmer for a few minutes until it slightly thickens.
9. Add the fried Lalmohon to the sugar syrup and let them soak for 10-15 minutes, allowing the syrup to penetrate the sweetmeats.

10. Once soaked, remove the Lalmohon from the syrup and arrange them on a serving plate.
11. Garnish with chopped nuts or dried fruits if desired.
12. Serve Lalmohon warm or at room temperature as a delightful sweet treat.

Enjoy the delicious and aromatic Lalmohon as a traditional Bangladeshi dessert!

Matha

Ingredients:

- 2 cups plain yogurt
- 2 cups water
- 1-2 tablespoons sugar (optional, adjust to taste)
- A pinch of salt (optional)
- A pinch of ground cumin powder (optional)
- Ice cubes (optional)
- Fresh mint leaves or cilantro leaves for garnish (optional)

Instructions:

1. In a blender, combine plain yogurt, water, sugar (if using), salt (if using), and ground cumin powder (if using).
2. Blend the ingredients until smooth and well combined. Taste and adjust the sweetness or saltiness according to your preference.
3. If you prefer a thinner consistency, you can add more water and blend again.
4. Pour the Matha into serving glasses.
5. If desired, add a few ice cubes to each glass to chill the Matha.
6. Garnish with fresh mint leaves or cilantro leaves, if using.
7. Serve Matha immediately as a refreshing beverage.

Enjoy the cool and tangy flavor of Matha as a delightful drink on a hot day or as a digestive after a meal!

Murighonto

Ingredients:

- 1 large fish head (such as rohu or katla), cleaned and chopped into pieces
- 1 cup red lentils (masoor dal), washed and soaked for 30 minutes
- 2-3 tablespoons mustard oil (or any cooking oil)
- 1 onion, finely chopped
- 2-3 green chilies, slit lengthwise (adjust to taste)
- 1 tablespoon ginger-garlic paste
- 1 teaspoon turmeric powder
- 1 teaspoon cumin powder
- 1 teaspoon coriander powder
- 1/2 teaspoon red chili powder (adjust to taste)
- Salt to taste
- Water, as needed
- Fresh cilantro leaves for garnish (optional)

Instructions:

1. Heat mustard oil in a large pot or pressure cooker over medium heat.
2. Add the chopped onion to the pot and sauté until it turns golden brown.
3. Add the slit green chilies and ginger-garlic paste to the pot. Sauté for another minute until the raw aroma disappears.
4. Add the chopped fish head pieces to the pot. Fry them for a few minutes until they start to brown slightly.
5. Drain the soaked lentils and add them to the pot along with turmeric powder, cumin powder, coriander powder, red chili powder, and salt. Mix well to coat the fish and lentils with the spices.
6. Add enough water to cover the fish and lentils. Bring the mixture to a boil.
7. Once boiling, reduce the heat to low and cover the pot. Let the Murighonto simmer for about 20-25 minutes, or until the lentils are cooked through and the fish is tender.
8. If using a pressure cooker, cook for about 2-3 whistles on medium heat.
9. Once cooked, check the seasoning and adjust salt if needed.
10. Garnish with fresh cilantro leaves, if desired.
11. Serve hot with steamed rice.

Enjoy the flavorful and hearty Murighonto as a comforting Bengali dish!

Narkel narus

Ingredients:

- 2 cups freshly grated coconut (you can use desiccated coconut as well)
- 1 cup sugar (adjust to taste)
- 1/2 teaspoon cardamom powder
- 2 tablespoons ghee (clarified butter)
- Chopped nuts (such as almonds, cashews, or pistachios) for garnish (optional)

Instructions:

1. Heat a non-stick pan or skillet over medium heat. Add the grated coconut to the pan and roast it for a few minutes until it becomes slightly dry and aromatic. Stir continuously to prevent burning.
2. Add the sugar to the pan with the roasted coconut. Mix well until the sugar starts to melt and combines with the coconut.
3. Add the ghee to the pan and mix well. Continue to cook the mixture, stirring frequently, until it thickens and starts to come together like a dough. This may take about 8-10 minutes.
4. Once the mixture reaches a dough-like consistency and starts to leave the sides of the pan, remove it from heat.
5. Add the cardamom powder to the mixture and mix well to incorporate.
6. Allow the mixture to cool down slightly until it's comfortable to handle.
7. Grease your palms with a little ghee and take small portions of the mixture. Roll each portion into small round balls or ladoos between your palms. Repeat this process with the remaining mixture.
8. If desired, garnish each Narkel Naru with chopped nuts by pressing them gently onto the surface.
9. Let the Narkel Narus cool completely at room temperature. Once cooled, store them in an airtight container.
10. Serve and enjoy these delicious Coconut Ladoos as a sweet treat!

Narkel Narus are perfect for sharing with family and friends or as a special homemade dessert for festive occasions.

Patisapta

Ingredients:

For the crepes:

- 1 cup all-purpose flour
- 1/2 cup semolina (sooji)
- 1 cup milk
- 1 cup water
- 2 tablespoons sugar
- A pinch of salt
- Ghee or oil for frying

For the filling:

- 1 cup grated coconut (fresh or desiccated)
- 1/2 cup khoya (milk solids)
- 1/2 cup sugar (adjust to taste)
- 1/4 teaspoon cardamom powder
- Chopped nuts (such as almonds, cashews, or pistachios) for garnish (optional)

Instructions:

1. To make the crepe batter, combine all-purpose flour, semolina, milk, water, sugar, and a pinch of salt in a mixing bowl. Whisk until you get a smooth batter without any lumps. The consistency should be similar to dosa or pancake batter. Let the batter rest for 15-20 minutes.
2. Meanwhile, prepare the filling. In a separate bowl, combine grated coconut, khoya, sugar, and cardamom powder. Mix well to form a smooth and slightly sticky mixture. Set aside.
3. Heat a non-stick or crepe pan over medium heat. Brush the surface with a little ghee or oil.
4. Pour a ladleful of the batter onto the pan and spread it evenly to form a thin crepe or pancake. Cook until the edges start to lift and the bottom is lightly golden brown.

5. Spoon some of the coconut and khoya filling onto one side of the crepe. Fold the other side over the filling to form a half-moon shape.
6. Gently press down on the edges to seal the crepe. Cook for another minute until the crepe is cooked through and golden brown on both sides.
7. Repeat the process with the remaining batter and filling.
8. Once all the Patisaptas are cooked, transfer them to a serving plate.
9. Garnish with chopped nuts, if desired.
10. Serve Patisapta warm or at room temperature as a delightful dessert.

Enjoy the delicious and aromatic Patisapta as a special treat during festive occasions or anytime you crave something sweet!

Sarson shorshe ilish

Ingredients:

- 4 pieces of Hilsa fish (Ilish), cleaned and washed
- 4 tablespoons mustard paste (made from ground mustard seeds)
- 2 tablespoons yogurt
- 2-3 green chilies, slit lengthwise
- 2 tablespoons mustard oil
- 1 tablespoon mustard seeds
- 1 teaspoon turmeric powder
- Salt to taste
- Fresh cilantro leaves for garnish (optional)

Instructions:

1. Marinate the Hilsa fish pieces with turmeric powder and a pinch of salt. Set aside for 15-20 minutes.
2. In a small bowl, mix the mustard paste with yogurt to form a smooth mixture.
3. Heat mustard oil in a pan over medium heat. Once the oil is hot, add mustard seeds and let them splutter.
4. Add the slit green chilies to the pan and sauté for a few seconds.
5. Reduce the heat to low and carefully add the marinated Hilsa fish pieces to the pan. Fry them gently on both sides until they turn golden brown. Remove the fish pieces from the pan and set aside.
6. In the same pan, add the mustard-yogurt mixture. Stir continuously to prevent lumps and cook for 2-3 minutes until the raw smell of mustard disappears and the mixture thickens slightly.
7. Add 1 cup of water to the pan and mix well to combine with the mustard-yogurt mixture.
8. Bring the gravy to a gentle simmer. Add salt to taste.
9. Carefully return the fried Hilsa fish pieces to the pan. Spoon some of the gravy over the fish pieces.
10. Cover the pan and let the fish cook in the gravy for 5-7 minutes, or until the fish is cooked through and the gravy thickens to your desired consistency.
11. Once done, remove the pan from heat.
12. Garnish with fresh cilantro leaves, if desired.
13. Serve Sarson Shorshe Ilish hot with steamed rice.

Enjoy the rich and flavorful Sarson Shorshe Ilish as a traditional Bengali delicacy!

Shahi tukda

Ingredients:

For the bread slices:

- 4-6 slices of white bread (preferably slightly stale)
- Ghee or oil for frying

For the sugar syrup:

- 1 cup sugar
- 1 cup water
- 2-3 green cardamom pods, crushed
- A few saffron strands (optional)
- A few drops of rose water or kewra water (optional)

For the rabri (thickened sweetened milk):

- 4 cups full-fat milk
- 1/2 cup sugar
- 1/2 teaspoon cardamom powder
- Chopped nuts (such as almonds, pistachios, and cashews) and dried fruits (such as raisins) for garnish

Instructions:

1. Start by preparing the sugar syrup. In a saucepan, combine sugar, water, crushed cardamom pods, and saffron strands (if using). Bring the mixture to a boil, then reduce the heat and let it simmer for 5-7 minutes until slightly thickened. Remove from heat and add rose water or kewra water if desired. Set aside to cool.
2. To make the rabri, pour the milk into a heavy-bottomed pan and bring it to a boil over medium heat. Once it comes to a boil, reduce the heat to low and let the milk simmer, stirring frequently to prevent sticking.
3. As the milk simmers and reduces, a thick layer of cream will form on top. Keep scraping the cream and adding it back to the milk. Continue to simmer until the milk reduces to about half its original volume and thickens to a creamy consistency.

4. Add sugar and cardamom powder to the thickened milk and mix well. Cook for another 5-10 minutes until the sugar dissolves completely and the rabri thickens further. Remove from heat and let it cool.
5. While the sugar syrup and rabri are cooling, prepare the bread slices. Trim the edges of the bread slices and cut them diagonally into triangles or squares.
6. Heat ghee or oil in a frying pan over medium heat. Fry the bread slices until they turn golden brown and crispy on both sides. Drain them on paper towels to remove excess oil.
7. Once the fried bread slices have cooled slightly, dip them into the sugar syrup for a few seconds, ensuring they are well soaked but not overly soggy. Place the soaked bread slices on a serving plate.
8. Spoon some of the prepared rabri over the soaked bread slices, covering them generously.
9. Garnish Shahi Tukda with chopped nuts and dried fruits.
10. Serve Shahi Tukda warm or chilled, as per your preference.

Enjoy the decadent and indulgent Shahi Tukda as a delightful dessert after your meal!

Sukto

Ingredients:

- 1 bitter gourd (karela), thinly sliced
- 1 small sweet potato, peeled and diced
- 1 small potato, peeled and diced
- 1 small eggplant (brinjal), diced
- 2-3 drumsticks (shojne data), cut into pieces
- 1 raw banana, peeled and diced
- 1 small radish, peeled and diced (optional)
- 1 cup pumpkin, diced (optional)
- 2 tablespoons mustard oil or vegetable oil
- 1 teaspoon mustard seeds
- 1/2 teaspoon fenugreek seeds
- 1/2 teaspoon nigella seeds (kalonji)
- 1/2 teaspoon turmeric powder
- 1 teaspoon ginger paste
- 1 teaspoon paanch phoron (Bengali five-spice blend)
- 2-3 green chilies, slit lengthwise
- 1 tablespoon grated coconut (optional)
- 1 tablespoon sugar or jaggery
- Salt to taste

Instructions:

1. Heat mustard oil or vegetable oil in a deep frying pan or kadhai over medium heat.
2. Add mustard seeds, fenugreek seeds, and nigella seeds to the hot oil. Let them splutter.
3. Add paanch phoron to the pan and sauté for a few seconds until aromatic.
4. Add the bitter gourd slices to the pan and sauté for 4-5 minutes until they start to soften.
5. Add the rest of the diced vegetables (sweet potato, potato, eggplant, drumsticks, raw banana, radish, and pumpkin) to the pan. Mix well with the sautéed bitter gourd.
6. Stir in turmeric powder and ginger paste. Mix well to coat the vegetables with the spices.
7. Add slit green chilies to the pan for heat, if desired.

8. Pour in enough water to cover the vegetables. Cover the pan and let the vegetables cook over low heat until they are tender.
9. Once the vegetables are cooked through, add grated coconut (if using) and sugar or jaggery to the pan. Mix well to combine.
10. Adjust the seasoning with salt to taste.
11. Let the Sukto simmer for a few more minutes until the flavors meld together.
12. Remove the pan from heat and transfer the Sukto to a serving dish.
13. Serve hot as a side dish with steamed rice.

Enjoy the unique flavors and textures of Sukto as part of a traditional Bengali meal!